the
every man
series

being God's man...
in the search for success

Stephen Arterburn

Kenny Luck & Todd Wendorff

WATERBROOK
PRESS

BEING GOD'S MAN...IN THE SEARCH FOR SUCCESS
PUBLISHED BY WATERBROOK PRESS
2375 Telstar Drive, Suite 160
Colorado Springs, Colorado 80920
A division of Random House, Inc.

ISBN 1-57856-680-0

Published in association with the literary agency of Alive Communications, Inc., 7680 Goddard Street, Suite 200, Colorado Springs, CO 80920.

Printed in the United States of America
2003—First Edition

10 9 8 7 6 5 4 3 2 1

contents

welcome to the every man
Bible study series

As Christian men, we crave true-to-life, honest, and revealing Bible study curricula that will equip us for the battles that rage in our lives. We are looking for resources that will get us into our Bibles in the context of mutually accountable relationships with other men. But like superheroes who wear masks and work hard to conceal their true identities, most of us find ourselves isolated and working alone on the major issues we face. Many of us present a carefully designed public self, while hiding our private self from view. This is not God's plan for us.

Let's face it. We all have trouble being honest with ourselves, particularly in front of other men.

As developers of a men's ministry, we believe that many of the problems among Christian men today are direct consequences of an inability to practice biblical openness—being honest about our struggles, questions, and temptations—and to connect with one another. Our external lives may be in order, but storms of unprocessed conflict, loss, and fear are eroding our resolve to maintain integrity. Sadly, hurting Christian men are flocking to unhealthy avenues of relief instead of turning to God's Word and to one another.

We believe the solution to this problem lies in creating opportunities for meaningful relationships among men. That's why we designed this Bible study series to be thoroughly interactive. When a man practices biblical openness with other men, he moves from secrecy to candor, from isolation to connection, and from pretense to authenticity.

Kenny and Todd developed the study sessions at Saddleback Church in Lake Forest, California, where they teach the men's morning Bible studies. There, men hear an outline of the Bible passage, read the verses together, and then answer a group discussion question at their small-group tables. The teaching pastor then facilitates further discussion within the larger group.

This approach is a huge success for many reasons, but the key is that, deep down, men really do want close friendships with other guys. We don't enjoy living on the barren islands of our own secret struggles. However, many men choose to process life, relationships, and pressures individually because they fear the vulnerability required in small-group gatherings. *Suppose someone sees behind my carefully constructed image? Suppose I encounter rejection after revealing one of my worst sins?* Men willingly take risks in business and the stock market, sports and recreation, but we do not easily risk our inner lives.

Many church ministries are now helping men win this battle, providing them with opportunities to experience Christian male companionship centered in God's Word. This study series aims to supplement and expand that good work around the country. If these lessons successfully reach you, then they will also reach every relationship and domain that you influence. That is our heartfelt prayer for every man in your group.

how to use this study guide

As you prepare for each session, first review the **Key Verse** and **Goals for Growth,** which reveal the focus of the study at hand. Discuss as a group whether or not you will commit to memorizing the Key Verse for each session. The **Head Start** section then explains why these goals are necessary and worthwhile. Each member of your small group should complete the **Connect with the Word** section *before* the small-group sessions. Consider this section to be your personal Bible study for the week. This will ensure that everyone has spent some time interacting with the biblical texts for that session and is prepared to share responses and personal applications. (You may want to mark or highlight any questions that were difficult or particularly meaningful, so you can focus on those during the group discussion.)

When you gather in your small group, you'll begin by reading aloud the **Head Start** section to remind everyone of the focus for the current session. The leader will then invite the group to share any questions, concerns, insights, or comments arising from their personal Bible study during the past week. If your group is large, consider breaking into subgroups of three or four people (no more than six) at this time.

Next get into **Connect with the Group,** starting with the **Group Opener.** These openers are designed to get at the heart of each week's lesson. They focus on how the men in your group relate to the passage and topic you are about to discuss. The group leader will read the opener for that week's session aloud and then facilitate interaction on the **Discussion Questions** that follow. (Remember: Not everyone has to offer an answer for every question.)

Leave time after your discussion to complete the **Standing Strong** exercises, which challenge each man to consider, *What's my next move?* As you openly express your thoughts to the group, you'll be able to hold one another accountable to reach for your goals.

Finally, close in **prayer,** either in your subgroups or in the larger group. You may want to use this time to reflect on and respond to what God has done in your group during the session. Also invite group members to share their personal joys and concerns, and use this as "grist" for your prayer time together.

By way of review, each lesson is divided into the following sections:

To be read or completed *before* the small-group session:
- **Key Verse**
- **Goals for Growth**
- **Head Start**
- **Connect with the Word** (home Bible study: 30-40 minutes)

To be completed *during* the small-group session:
- Read aloud the **Head Start** section (5 minutes)
- Discuss personal reaction to **Connect with the Word** (10 minutes)
- **Connect with the Group** (includes the **Group Opener** and discussion of the heart of the lesson: 30-40 minutes)
- **Standing Strong** (includes having one person pray for the group; challenges each man to take action: 20 minutes)

redefining success

David's life epitomized worldly success. He made it to the top—rising from shepherd boy to king of the most powerful army of the Middle East. Yet who would have imagined that the forgotten son of a sheepherder would outperform his brothers and peers to become the most powerful and influential king of the nation of Israel? No one messed with King David's army or kingdom. Like Pharaoh or the Hittite king Pithana, David reached mega-king status.

Although most men won't achieve the kind of success David did, many of us will become successful in some area of our lives. It might be in our careers, in sending a couple of kids off to college, in walking a daughter down the aisle, or in celebrating a twenty-fifth wedding anniversary with our bride. That's success! But no matter how good it is to be successful in these areas, it's more important that we understand how God defines success. Worldly success is tied to position, power, and wealth, but godly success is all about knowing God intimately and living for Him regardless of our status in life. (See Jeremiah 9:23-24.) A man may be a failure in the eyes of the world, but a success in God's eyes. On the other hand, a man may experience great worldly success, but how he handles it reveals what kind of man he is from God's perspective.

How do you respond to success when it comes? Will you look back and think that everything you accomplished was by your own sweat and toil? Or will you see the hand of the Lord in your life, behind the scenes, constantly helping you become everything you are? Like any proud father, God loves it when we do well, but He loves it more when we demonstrate humility in the midst of our success.

If only David had learned that lesson. As he moved from one success to another, he fell prey to pride, self-reliance, and eventually defeat. Don't let this happen to you! Learn from David. Sometimes he got it right. Sometimes he got it wrong.

Success is a double-edged blade. If you handle it improperly, it will cut you. It's not something to be handled carelessly. And like being cut by a razor blade, you won't even know you're bleeding until you've got a mess on your hands. It can happen to any one of us. What will you do if you receive a raise or a promotion? Will everything change? Will you flaunt your success? Or will you continue driving the same car, eating at the same places, and treating people the same way you always did? Be careful!

Our goal in this study is to stimulate personal reflection and honest dialogue with God and with other men about these matters. As you work through each session, look in the mirror at your own life and ask yourself some hard questions. Whether you are doing this study individually or in a group, realize that complete honesty with yourself, with God, and with others will produce the greatest results.

Our prayer is that you will be moved to embrace God's perspective on success in a way that produces a kingdom-honoring legacy of faith in your life. If that is your prayer as well, then welcome aboard!

where success starts

Key Verse

David was greatly distressed because the men were talking of stoning him; each one was bitter in spirit because of his sons and daughters. But David found strength in the LORD his God. (1 Samuel 30:6)

Goals for Growth

- Recognize our true source of help in the midst of trouble.
- Understand what it means to seek God's help and strength.
- Realize the possible sources of help that God may provide.

Head Start

Most men want success. We want it in our jobs, in our homes, and with our finances. Some men want it so badly that they are willing to pay any price for it. Unfortunately, their pursuit of success comes at great expense as they neglect other areas of their lives. Some men will even sacrifice their families for a successful career. Others will give up on spiritual growth.

How does a godly man achieve the kind of success God values? He begins by eliminating pride and replacing it with humility. That's hard to do.

David went from zero to hero, and then from hero to zero. At first, David was a nobody, working as a sheepherder for his father, Jesse. Then David was anointed as the future king of Israel. Later he slayed Goliath and was drafted into royal service. David had great success as a warrior, but when Saul turned against him, even that was taken away. The minute David had it all, he lost it. He had no job, no tangible purpose in life. And he was depressed. He became a fugitive running from King Saul, a man bent on killing him. Later, he appeared to be a traitor when he fled to the Philistines because he felt it was the only way he could keep himself—and his six hundred men and their families—safe.

David faced many tests of his character on the road to success. But he learned that success always comes with a series of tests. David's dilemma was the same as ours: He had to choose how he was going to respond to events in the heat of the moment. David's response to rejection and defeat won him success. For instance, when the Philistines refused to let David go into battle with them, he went home only to find that the Amalekites had pillaged and burned his base camp and had kidnapped all the women and children. His country had been compromised, and the people had lost faith in his ability to lead. (See 1 Samuel 29:1–30:6.) Could David have experienced a more gut-wrenching defeat? Yet David eventually found success, regained control of his city, and won back the confidence of the people.

When you're pushed up against a wall, how do you react? When people or circumstances turn against you and you are being blamed, how do you respond? Do you get defensive? Do you come out with both guns blazing? Do you excuse? accuse? rationalize your behavior? withdraw? run? All of these responses are signs of a weak character and will eventually result in defeat. It is never God's will for you to run from your problems. Rather, God wants you to rely on Him—not on feelings—and to take the practical steps within your power to deal with your problems.

So will you pursue success your way or God's way?

Connect with the Word

Read 1 Samuel 30.

1. According to verses 1-4, why was the attack on Ziklag so devastating for David and his men?

2. How did David's men react to this tragedy? How did David react?

3. What thoughts and feelings do you think David was battling as he looked around at his circumstances?

4. What enabled David to keep on going? Where did he find strength?

5. What would seeking God's direction and strength in your daily life or in your times of trouble look like?

6. When you find yourself under pressure, what are you tempted to do? Where are you tempted to turn?

7. What do you do when you haven't been given a game plan that shows you how to move ahead? What did David do (verses 6-8)?

8. We don't use an ephod today, but what do you think God expects us to do when we need help? (See 1 Samuel 23:2; 30:8.)

Note: An ephod is a sacred garment made of fine linen and gold, and of blue, purple, and scarlet yarn. (See Exodus 28:4-14.) The Jewish high priest wore this garment to seek God's will for the nation of Israel. It signified the people's dependence upon God for His help and strength in times of great distress and spiritual need.

9. According to verses 9-16, in what form did help come to David and his men? Describe a time, if any, when God sent you help from an unlikely and unexpected source in a time of trouble.

10. What do we learn about David's character from his treatment of the slave?

11. How do you think David's responses under pressure strengthened his position as heir to the throne of Israel?

12. When David reflected on his actions during this period of time, how do you think he felt about himself?

Connect with the Group

Group Opener
(Suggestion: As you begin your group discussion time in each of the following sessions, consider forming smaller groups of three to six men. This will allow more time for discussion and give everyone an opportunity to share their thoughts and struggles.)

How do the difficulties we face contribute to our success? Share a specific example, if you can.

Discussion Questions

a. How has David handled the losses in his life from the time he left Jonathan until now? What progress or growth have you seen? What does this tell you about what God was doing in David's character?

b. Why do you think we so easily resort to blaming others for our troubles just as David's men blamed him? (See 1 Samuel 30:1-6.) How does this kind of response hinder success?

c. In what ways does David's example show us how to deal with the crushing blows of defeat in our lives. (See 1 Samuel 30:7-8.)

d. What circumstances are you facing for which you need to seek the Lord's guidance and strength? Ask a couple of the men to share what they have learned from God's Word about how to handle defeat in a way that demonstrates godly character.

Standing Strong

Complete the following statement based upon what you have learned about how God wants you to deal with your struggles or defeats.

The man after God's own heart _____.

What one area of your life are you struggling with right now?

Have you humbled yourself and really asked God for His help, strength, and direction with your struggle? Read Micah 6:8 and spend time coming humbly before God each morning this week. If necessary, commit to getting up ten minutes earlier each day.

the success test: defeating pride

Key Verse

When all the elders of Israel had come to King David at Hebron, the king made a compact with them at Hebron before the LORD, and they anointed David king over Israel. (2 Samuel 5:3)

Goals for Growth

- Recognize that worldly success leaves us vulnerable to forgetting about God.
- Realize God is responsible for our successes.
- Honor God in the midst of our successes.

Head Start

The moment has arrived. David is finally king. Saul is dead, but so is David's close friend Jonathan. After seven years of civil unrest in

Israel, David reunites a torn country and takes the throne. But now that David is king, will he let success go to his head?

Scripture says that David's kingdom grew greater and greater. (See 2 Samuel 8.) He defeated the Philistines. He acquired concubines. Then David wanted the ultimate symbol of national unity—the ark—in his own city. What's wrong with that? Nothing—unless you take matters into your own hands to get what you want.

The greatest threat to a man's character is success. If it goes to his head, it's lethal. Success started going to David's head. He began to think his accomplishments were the result of his own efforts and abilities. When a man begins to think this way, he fails to give God credit, and his perspective shifts away from God's infinite goodness and provision to his own fallible personhood. That's always dangerous.

How would success ultimately affect David, the man after God's own heart? Would God become an afterthought to him? Would he lose all the growth in character that he had experienced? Would he pass the success test?

We can glean some valuable lessons from this time of titanic change in the life of David, because we ourselves are the most vulnerable to sin and spiritual failure during times of success. Would David push too hard? Would he run ahead of God?

Connect with the Word

Read 2 Samuel 5:1-13.

1. According to verses 12 and 13, what impact did David's rise to power have on him? What warning and instruction is given in

Deuteronomy 17:17 to one who would rule as king over Israel? What was the danger? What evidence do we see in our own lives that this warning is valid?

2. What did David know about how and why he had come to power (verse 12)? Do you think David had proper attitudes about his success? Why or why not?

3. What attitudes help produce a godly response to victory, success, promotion, and increased responsibility? What can we do to develop these attitudes?

4. What dangerous perspectives might we have when we possess much or very little? (*Hint:* See Proverbs 30:7-9.)

Read 2 Samuel 5:17-25.

5. In David's first days as king, he was tested with a crisis. According to verse 19, what was his first reaction?

6. How did God respond to David's request? What was the result of David's obedience to God?

7. In what circumstance in your life have you sensed a clear "go" from God (verse 19)?

8. Where can we get clear direction from God? How can we be sure that it really has come from God?

9. Not long after David and his men defeated the Philistines, the Philistines came back. What does it mean when a problem resurfaces? What does David's example tell us about how to deal with recurring problems?

Read 2 Samuel 6:1-23.

10. The ark of the covenant contained the Word of God (the Ten Commandments God gave Moses), written on tablets of stone. What did David learn about the ark in verse 12? (*Note:* For further insight about the incident described in verses 1–7, read 1 Chronicles 15:11-15 and note what David later discovered about the right way to move the ark.)

11. When David brought the ark into Jerusalem, what did his thoughts seem to be focused on? In what ways was his thinking good? bad?

12. Keep in mind that David wanted a good thing. He wanted the ark of the covenant, which represented God's Word and presence, to be in Jerusalem. But his motives were not entirely pure. He was rushing God. Do you seek God with mixed motives? Do you have a tendency to rush God to get what you want? Explain.

Connect with the Group

Group Opener

Pride isn't easy to detect. It subtly invades our hearts and minds and begins to influence our choices.

Here's a quick test. Are you:

___talking too much about yourself?

___rarely asking other people questions about themselves?

___focusing on your own needs and wants?

___thinking you can get away with sin in your life?

___not feeling the need to spend time in the Word and in prayer?

___ selectively obeying God's Word?

When you are on top and experiencing success, in what ways can your relationship with God change? Share a personal story, if you can.

Discussion Questions

a. Generally speaking, how well do you think David handled his long-awaited success? Explain.

b. In what ways does the Enemy use worldly success to tempt us not to be fully dependent on God?

c. Read Proverbs 30:7-9 together as a group. What attitude should we have about possessions? What should our response be to achieving success and the desires of our hearts?

d. Reflect on the passages presented in this session. Based on these passages, what do you think David did right? What do you think he did wrong?

Standing Strong

Complete the following sentence based on what you learned in this session about how to deal with pride.

The man after God's own heart _____.

How are you doing with recognizing that what you have—your success, material gain, position, and influence—all come from God? Do you need to surrender to God your sense of accomplishment (or even your sense of failure) and allow Him to assume His rightful place of control in your life? Pray for one another and ask God to help you humble yourselves before Him and relinquish control to Him.

being flexible when God says no

Key Verse

O Sovereign LORD, you are God! Your words are trustworthy, and you have promised these good things to your servant. (2 Samuel 7:28)

Goals for Growth

- Recognize that David trusted God even when He said no.
- Recognize that God rewarded David's right attitude.
- Commit to an attitude about circumstances that pleases God.

Head Start

How do you respond when God says no—when you're passed up for a promotion...when a deal falls through...when financial relief won't come...when your spouse won't change...when your kids won't listen to you...when you're not getting what you expected out of life?

We can become discouraged and depressed, or we can focus on God's purpose in our circumstances. A no from God is not a dead end, but a new direction. Behind every no is an opportunity to respond to the Lord with faith and enthusiasm.

That's what David did. With all the inauguration ceremonies over, all the cabinet positions filled, and peace in his kingdom, David dreamed of building a temple for his God. He thought it was the right time and place and that he was the right person, but God had other plans. David's son Solomon would be the builder instead.

David's dream was shattered, but this didn't mean he was out of the game. God gave him another role: making all the necessary preparations for building the temple. David responded in faith and humbly accepted his role. Can we begin responding this way in our own lives when God says no?

Second Samuel 7–9 paints several pictures that show how God's man embraced the work God had called him to do. It may not have been what David had expected to do, but it was still God's plan. How did he set about his work? How did he pray? How did he handle his power and position? How did he serve others? In this session we will see the shepherd-warrior-king at his best.

Connect with the Word

Read 2 Samuel 7:1-17.

1. David's kingdom was settled, but what was David's concern in verse 2? Where did he think he needed to be directing his energy?

2. What was the essence of Nathan's reply to David's observation (verse 3)?

3. Why do you think God provided this time of calm in David's life? How often do you set aside time to take an inventory of your life?

4. When we desire to do something for God, what should our response be—regardless of whether He says yes or no?

5. In what way did God reward the desire of David's heart?

Read 2 Samuel 7:18-29.

6. Based on verses 18-21, how do you think David viewed himself?

7. What was the main message of David's prayer to God in verses 18-29?

8. What did David desire even more than building a dwelling for God (verses 25 and 26)?

9. How was David affected by God's promise concerning his future (verse 27)?

10. What did David believe about God that allowed him to trust Him (verse 28)?

11. What things tend to prevent you from completely trusting in God? What would help you gain more trust?

Read 2 Samuel 8:1-15; 9:1-3.

12. How do you think David was able to stay focused on God in the face of his success?

13. Why do you think that, at the height of his power, David was concerned about the descendants of Saul and Jonathan? (See 1 Samuel 20:14-17.)

14. When have you had the opportunity to show concern toward someone you really didn't have to pay attention to? Describe your experience.

Connect with the Group

Group Opener

Read the group opener aloud and discuss the questions that follow.

Jesus is the poster boy of the undivided heart, our model role model. From His undivided heart flowed the deep waters of conviction and spiritual integrity, which fostered and fed the growth of the strongest spine in human history....

As one of my favorite authors, Brennan Manning, puts it, "His doing and his being, like his divinity and humanity, were one." His identity in His Father was formed in His heart in such a way that the world saw a real man. One who was free to love, help, heal, serve, teach, confront, and connect radically with people. Most important for us males, Jesus Christ modeled how to release oneself fully to God's purposes in the face of personal suffering—the real test of a man's heart.

On the night before He died, Jesus took Peter, James, and John with Him on an occasion when He was deeply distressed about His situation. "My soul is overwhelmed with sorrow to the point of death," He told His friends. While they proceeded to doze off, Jesus fell to the ground and prayed that, if possible, the inevitability of the cross could somehow be altered:

"Abba, Father," he said, "everything is possible for you. Take this cup from me. Yet not what I will, but what you will." (Mark 14:36)

Jesus knew what was coming, and the human side wanted out. He was honest and real. But instead of longing for a way out, He committed His heart to God's purposes for Him and gave every one of us His undivided loyalty.... The most important thing Jesus might have ever shown us was how to completely let go of our hearts to God. And that He did. But He also stiffened His spine. Spine comes from undivided trust in the One who gave us the undivided heart. There is no sadder or more pathetic man than the one with a heart but no spine.[1]

---

1. Stephen Arterburn and Kenny Luck, *Every Man, God's Man* (Colorado Springs: WaterBrook Press, 2003), 29-30.

Discussion Questions

a. When have you sensed that God was giving you a tough but definite no? How did you react?

b. In what ways does Jesus' example encourage you? make you uncomfortable?

c. What do you think David did well as the new king of Israel?

d. What areas in David's life do you see as potential stress fractures or breaking points?

e. Why was David able to accept God's refusal to allow him to build the temple?

f. How are we able to reconcile what we *desire* from God with what we *actually get* in life?

Standing Strong

Complete the following sentence in light of what you've learned in this study about how to respond when God says no.

The man after God's own heart _____.

David's relationship with and trust in God enabled him to keep a right attitude in difficult circumstances. In what area(s) of your life do you need to trust God more completely and accept His yes or no answer with a right heart attitude? What changes do you need to make in how you respond to God?

a heart for people in the midst of our success

Key Verse

The LORD gave David victory wherever he went. David reigned over all Israel, doing what was just and right for all his people. (2 Samuel 8:14-15)

Goals for Growth

- Learn how King David reached out to people at the height of his success.
- Consider what we can do for others in God's strength.
- Commit to following Jesus' example of compassion.

Head Start

Most conquering kings in the Bible don't come across as sensitive, caring people. They don't tend to focus on the condition and welfare of individuals, but on consolidation of power and accumulation of possessions. It's about kicking booty and getting booty.

When a man becomes powerful, it is rare to find him extending compassion to others along the way. Success usually comes by steam-rolling over others. Yet David displayed an unusual heart for people in the midst of his military successes. His sense of responsibility to shepherd his people marked him as a truly successful man.

Unfortunately, we don't often view success that way.

But if we want to be God's man, we will see our accomplishments as secondary and how we use them to influence and care for people as primary. Jesus, a reigning king Himself, said in Mark 10:45 that "even the Son of Man did not come to be served, but to serve, and to give his life as a ransom for many."

In a very short period of time, David had defeated the Philistines, the Moabites, the King of Zobah, the Arameans, and the Edomites. David made a name for himself; he topped all the popularity polls and was enjoying the zenith of his power and influence. But how would David use that power?

Connecting with the Word

Read 2 Samuel 8–9.

1. How are David's victories described in 8:1-14? Whom did David conquer?

2. Based upon your study of chapter 8, why do you think David pursued his military duty so aggressively?

3. What does it mean that David "made a name for himself" (8:13, NASB)?

4. Have you ever made a name for yourself? What effect did this have on your personality? your actions? your spiritual life?

5. How did David use the power and influence he gained from his military successes (8:15)? In what ways was his kindness and compassion for the people demonstrated?

6. What do you think was behind David's military successes and his heart for people (8:6,14)?

7. In chapter 9, how did David show kindness to the people in his kingdom?

8. Do you think David's compassion went too far (9:13)? Why or why not?

Connect with the Group

Group Opener

In what ways are we as men called to be great conquerors and caring servants like David? Describe a time in your life when you most powerfully felt that calling.

Discussion Questions

a. In what ways does God's man go beyond obligation and good manners to show Jesus-like compassion for others? As a group, brainstorm some practical actions you might take.

b. How should we deal with those who need our help but refuse it? Share with the group any such situations you may have encountered in your life.

Standing Strong

List some specific ways you have demonstrated kindness and compassion to others in the past.

Have you ever been unkind or uncaring toward someone? As a result of this study, what will you do to treat people differently in the future?

too proud to see it coming

Key Verse

One evening David got up from his bed and walked around on the roof of the palace. From the roof he saw a woman bathing. The woman was very beautiful. (2 Samuel 11:2)

Goals for Growth

- Observe the progression of David's sin.
- Recognize our own vulnerability to moral failure.
- Make a plan to prevent the progress of sin in our own lives.

Head Start

David was solidly in the saddle. He had more military victories under his belt than any other king. He had successfully united the kingdom of Israel under one ruler. Peace, prosperity, and power surrounded him. Was David untouchable? Hardly. In the midst of such great success, God's man was extremely vulnerable. At a time when he should have gone to war with his army, David stayed back. He became idle. He also became isolated and therefore susceptible to attack. And this idleness and isolation led David to commit grievous sins for which he paid dearly.

How could a man after God's own heart fall so far? He had survived the rampages of Saul's persecution. He had sought after God. He had fought long and hard to ensure that his kindom was secure from its enemies. Yet David was not perfect. In at least one area of his life—sexual integrity—he had not been fully tested. Sadly, when temptation came, he gave in to his lust. Subsequently, he seemed to care more about self-preservation and self-promotion than about bringing glory to God. He even compromised his integrity and tested the boundaries of God's will for his life. There is no greater shame for a man than to lose his sexual integrity—and no greater loss for the one betrayed. David's moral failure had far-reaching consequences that affected many others.

Learning how to control our own sinful appetites and avoid the circumstances that trigger our compulsions is critical to our success in becoming God's man. If we discipline ourselves and work to master our own flesh, we will experience less of God's discipline and more of His success in our lives.

Connect with the Word

Read 2 Samuel 11:1-5.

1. What details in verse 1 indicate that it was not a normal occurrence for David to stay in Jerusalem during this time? What

spiritual insights can you glean from the situation presented in this verse?

2. What sequence of events described in verses 2 and 3 signify David's progression toward failure as he faced sexual temptation?

3. What does sexual temptation look like in our own lives today? Give some specific examples.

4. As men, what do we need to do to resist the lure of this kind of temptation? Be specific.

Read 2 Samuel 11:6-27.

5. Briefly describe the actions David took that plunged him deeper into sin, deception, and moral failure.

6. List each circumstance or decision that David faced, and write one word to describe the sin or driving force behind David's actions. Pay particular attention to the actions described in verses 4-8,13, and 14-15. For example:
   • "David got up…and walked…on the roof."—Boredom
   • "[David] saw a woman bathing."—Lust

7. What do you think was going on in David's mind as he was living out this chain of events?

8. How should knowing what God thinks about self-deception, lies, and sin affect our behavior?

9. What insight do you gain about David's conscience in verse 27? Do you think David felt as if the issue was over for him? Why or why not?

Read 2 Samuel 12:1-7,13.

10. When David heard the prophet Nathan's story, he became angry. How do you think David felt when Nathan said, "You are the man" (verse 7)?

11. What was David's response to Nathan (verse 13)? What do David's words tell you about the condition of his heart before God at that moment?

12. When God confronts the deep-seated sin in our lives, what is the best response we can have?

13. What does it take for you to live a life of sexual integrity today?

Connect with the Group

Group Opener
Read the group opener aloud and discuss the questions that follow.

At a men's retreat, my church surveyed 550 men by asking the following question: What causes you to disconnect from God on a continual, habitual, or fatal basis?

More than 90 percent of the men indicated (anonymously) that lust, porn, and sexual fantasy were their top reasons for spiritual disconnection. Many men took advantage of the survey's anonymity to reveal their involvement in love affairs, their compulsive addiction to pornography, and the inner struggles that plagued their consciences and drained their spirits. Shockingly, more than fifty men at the retreat admitted that they were having—or had had—an extramarital affair. Equally shocking was the fact that the majority of the men were serving in key leadership positions throughout the church. One man told a familiar story:

> I know it's wrong. I know I shouldn't do that, say that, or watch that. It feels wrong, but I do it anyway. I always say to myself that I'll start all over tomorrow. Just one more day, then I'll start over on Monday. I can change. I'll just do it later.

Intellectually and mentally, this fellow knows God's standard for such behavior. Practically and experientially, however, he's experienced an erosion of character that is failing to stop the landslides of failure.[2]

---

2. Stephen Arterburn and Kenny Luck, *Every Man, God's Man* (Colorado Springs: WaterBrook Press, 2003), 33-4.

Discussion Questions

a. What is your reaction to the 90 percent statistic in the survey?

b. What can a man do to stop the "landslides of failure" in the area of sexual temptation? What helps or hinders you?

c. What are some of the sources of sexual temptation that men today struggle with?

d. What are some of the ways we use sin to ease the pain of past hurts? What is a better way of dealing with our pain?

e. At what point do you think it might have been possible for David to prevent his sin (described in 2 Samuel 11:1-4)?

f. As a group, brainstorm some preventive measures we can take
to keep ourselves from falling into the same trap David did.

Standing Strong

Complete the following statement based on what God has shown
you in this study about dealing with sexual temptation.

The man after God's own heart _____.

In what area of your life are you most vulnerable to moral failure?
What do you need to change in order to protect yourself from falling
into this kind of sin?

Write down the name of a friend on whom you can count to speak
the truth to you when you need to hear it. If you need to develop this
kind of friendship, what steps can you take to get started?

confronting personal sin

Key Verse

David said to Nathan, "I have sinned against the LORD." (2 Samuel 12:13)

Goals for Growth

- Recognize the appropriate steps to take to confront sin.
- Understand the benefits of accountability.
- Commit to finding an accountability partner.

Head Start

Success often gives us a false sense of self-sufficiency. How quickly we fall into temptation and sin when we stop seeking God and start calling the shots ourselves! Before we know it, we are making a mess of our lives and relationships. To our shame, we make things worse when we try to cover up our mistakes, deny that they even exist, rationalize them away so that we can live with ourselves, or blame others for "making" us choose sin.

David was in this ugly and destructive place. He had decided he deserved a break, so he skipped out on his responsibilities. He was not where he was supposed to be, and he had no constructive plan for how to spend his time. In addition, he seemed to be unconnected and unaccountable to other people. Isolated and bored, he was susceptible to the deadly allure of sin.

He also put Bathsheba in a no-win situation, using his power and position to gratify his selfish appetite. Then in his efforts to protect his secret, he lost his ability to care about others or to act in a manner pleasing to God. He had gone from being a man above reproach to being the scum of the earth. Can you imagine how he felt?

Running for cover, our once-noble king engineered a plot to cover his tracks. David arranged for Bathsheba's husband, Uriah, to come home from battle and sleep with his wife. David hoped that making it look as if the baby had been produced from an evening of marital passion between Bathsheba and her husband would take care of the problem. However, the honorable Uriah foiled the plot when he refused these luxuries while his men were still on the battlefield.

David's sin reached new depths when he placed Uriah in the heaviest fighting in hopes that he would be killed. His response to Uriah's death was callous and businesslike. What happened to the man who had grieved so deeply over the death of his enemies, Saul and Absalom? Sin had hardened David's heart and made him insensitive to both God and man.

Thank God for Nathan! With courage and commitment, he confronted David and exposed his sin. But how would David respond?

Connect with the Word

Read 2 Samuel 12:1-14.

1. What was Nathan's responsibility to David as a prophet of God?

2. Why do you think he confronted David the way he did (verses 1-4)?

3. Based on Matthew 7:1-5 and Galatians 6:1-5, what is the appropriate way to confront someone who is sinning?

4. What do we learn from Nathan's example about the importance of having an accountability partner?

5. What indication do you find in verse 13 that David responded biblically when he was confronted with his sin?

6. What do you learn from Psalm 32:5, James 5:16, and 1 John 1:9 about what God requires of us when we sin?

7. According to verses 10 and 14, what were the consequences of David's sin?

8. God does not usually protect us from consequences when we sin. What are some of the possible consequences that we could face?

9. List some ineffective ways of confronting others with their sin. What can we learn about how to confront others from Nathan's example?

10. How is accepting responsibility for our mistakes a sign of success? Explain.

11. What do you see in David's confession that seems to indicate that his repentance was sincere and complete rather than partial and insincere?

12. What do you think are the steps to true repentance?

Connect with the Group

Group Opener
Share some reasons why confronting sin in our own lives and in the lives of others is so uncomfortable. When have you experienced such confrontation as a great blessing?

Discussion Questions
a. Why do you think Nathan was willing to risk his relationship with David by confronting the king's sin? (See Proverbs 27:5-6.)

b. Why do you think David was so upset by Nathan's story? What do we learn from this example about our own tendency to cover up sin?

c. How could David have dealt with his own sin rather than having to be confronted by Nathan? What steps are necessary to truly deal with the sin in our lives?

d. What do you think it would mean to have an accountability relationship with another man? What might some of the benefits be?

e. How do we go about finding an accountability partner—and being one?

Standing Strong

Complete the following sentence based on what you have learned this week about accountability and confronting sin.

The man after God's own heart _____.

Is there an area of struggle in your life for which you need to be held accountable? Write about it below. Take a step of courage and share your struggle with a trusted brother.

recovering from the fallout of sin

Key Verse

Because by doing this you have made the enemies of the LORD show utter contempt, the son born to you will die. (2 Samuel 12:14)

Goals for Growth

- Realize that God forgives us when we confess our sins.
- Recognize that God does not remove the consequences of our sin.
- See that God's call on our lives remains despite our failures.

Head Start

Success often gives rise to pride and many other sins. How we handle our sin in the midst of success reveals the kind of men we are and determines who we will become. After we've repented of our sin, the critical factor then becomes how we deal with the inevitable consequences.

We have learned from David's calamity, Nathan's confrontation, and David's sincere repentance that we can begin again, even after significant failure. But we also see in the aftermath of this event in David's life that sinful choices produce painful consequences and ongoing grief. Guilt, bitterness, shame, loss of a child, loss of affection, loss of relationship, and loss of credibility and reputation are just some of the consequences that David experienced as a result of his sin. His family suffered, and he experienced increasing difficulty ruling over his kingdom.

Whether our sin is invisible to outsiders or titanic in scale and publicly humiliating, all of us need to deal with the consequences of our sin in a way that pleases God. When we make a mess of our lives and the lives of others, we need to, as Jesus said in Matthew 3:8, "Produce fruit in keeping with repentance."

Sadly, straightening out our lives isn't easy, and the bumpy road we're now traveling may never become completely smooth again this side of heaven.

Even so, we can choose whether we will dwell on our past sin, wallow in guilt, and stagnate or—as David did—begin again, make amends, and use our pain to create, renew, or clarify our mission in life.

As we'll see in this session, life sometimes gets worse before it gets better. But God uses each experience in our lives to accomplish His plans for us in our search for godly success.

Connect with the Word

Read 2 Samuel 12:14-21.

Look up the following verses in 2 Samuel that describe the catastrophic results of David's sin.

- 12:18—David's son died.
- 13:11-14—Amnon, David's son, committed incest.
- 15:1-12—Absalom, David's son, led a revolt against King David.
- 16:6—Inhabitants of the land threw stones at King David.
- 18:14-15—Absalom died.
- 20:5—Disobedience to the king became evident.
- 21:1—Famine came to the land.
- 21:15-16—David became weary.

1. What are your initial thoughts concerning the gravity of David's sin and its consequences in the lives of his family and kingdom?

2. Why do you think God judged David and his kingdom so harshly?

3. Have you seen the effects of your sin in your relationship with God and with others, maybe even within your own family? Explain.

4. What insight does Numbers 14:18 offer regarding the effects of sin on our families?

5. As David experienced the consequences of his sin, he humbly turned to God in prayer. What does this tell you about the sincerity of David's repentance? (See 2 Samuel 12:20-23; 13:31; 15:25-26.)

6. According to 2 Samuel 12:24, what good did God bring into David's life after his sin with Bathsheba?

7. In verse 5, David himself said he deserved death for his sin. Why do you think God blessed David instead of killing him?

8. What compels God to continue blessing us even when our sin is as grievous as David's?

9. Do you see any conditions attached to receiving God's blessing? In what way(s) did David's response in verse 13 seem to satisfy or please God?

10. In what ways can living in the past—and constantly reliving our failures—affect our relationship with God? What do we need to do to get right with God again and live the life He has called us to?

11. What, if any, deep loss due to sin or hardship are you hanging on to? What impact is it having on your current relationships?

Connect with the Group

Group Opener
Read the group opener aloud and discuss the questions that follow.

Practically speaking, if a man loves God and is doing everything we've presented in this book, but he's still in bondage to a particular hang-up or habit, that's a sign to us that there is still some unfinished business in need of God's healing touch. Past hurts motivate present behavior, and the man's relationships—including his connection to God—will be negatively influenced by those hurts until the root causes are discovered, acknowledged, and brought to Him.

Only the bravest of God's men go there. Why? Because it means examining some painful truths we would rather forget.[3]

---

3. Stephen Arterburn and Kenny Luck, *Every Man, God's Man* (Colorado Springs: WaterBrook Press, 2003), 204.

Discussion Questions

a. What is your reaction to the group opener? Do you agree or disagree? Explain.

b. In what ways does this opener personally challenge you as a Christian man?

c. Why do you think God takes even trivial sins in our lives so seriously?

d. Why is anger so often our first reaction when we have made a mess of our lives? Where do we typically direct this anger?

e. In what ways does accepting responsibility for our behavior change our reaction to sin and its consequences? Why do you think it is so difficult for us to accept responsibility for our behavior?

f. Share with the group any encouragement you have gained from David's open admission of sin against God when Nathan confronted him.

g. How did David deal with the consequences of sin in his life? What would it look like to follow David's example when facing the consequences of our sin?

h. Take turns reading through Psalm 51 aloud. In what ways does prayer become the way of a repentant heart?

Standing Strong

Complete the following sentence based on what you have learned this week about recovering from the fallout of sin.

The man after God's own heart _____.

Confessing our sins to God—and to one another—is the first step in restoring a right relationship with Him and with others. Is there any sin in your life that you need to take responsibility for and confess to God and to a trusted friend? Think of at least one person with whom you can share your story and who will hold you accountable as you seek to restore your relationship with God. Write that person's name below.

finishing well

Key Verses

You, my son Solomon, acknowledge the God of your father, and serve him with wholehearted devotion and with a willing mind, for the LORD searches every heart and understands every motive behind the thoughts. If you seek him, he will be found by you; but if you forsake him, he will reject you forever. (1 Chronicles 28:9)

Goals for Growth

- Understand that true success is living a life of wholehearted devotion to God and finishing well.
- Seek to leave a legacy that honors God and influences others.
- Recognize that ability will get you results, but godly character yields eternal rewards.

Head Start

A seminary professor once said, "There are two problems with leaders today. They don't replace themselves, and they don't finish well."

Success is about finishing well. David desired to finish well. What about you?

God chose David to be king because his heart was right before God. (See 1 Samuel 16:7.) In our study, we have seen David respond to his circumstances with humility before God as well as with pride and independence. We have also seen how humility and reliance on God can cause a man to rise to heights he never dreamed of, and how pride can undo him in a millisecond.

Humility was the key to David's development as a man and as a man after God's own heart. Hardship was the key to the maturity of David's character and his growth as a leader. When his pride tricked him into independence, he became a hard, hollow, and humiliated leader. The backwash of David's sin lingered around him for decades in the form of incest, murder, and rebellion. But David endured and ultimately did what was right before God.

David began well by focusing his eyes on the Lord. (See 1 Samuel 17:37,45-47.) He made mistakes and had great moral and personal failures, but in the end, David rediscovered his passion for being a man of God and set his focus on finishing well. That's success.

As a general, a king, a father, and a man after God's own heart, David focused on his comeback. He did not want to leave a legacy of defeat. If he was going to fail, he would fail with both guns blazing, as Teddy Roosevelt said, "while daring greatly so that his place will not rest with those timid souls who knew neither victory nor defeat." The final chapter of David's life challenges all men to finish well by living a life focused on God.

Connect with the Word

Read 1 Chronicles 28:1-10.

1. David charged his son Solomon, all the officials of Israel, and all the people with the task of building God's temple. As he began, David reflected on the loss of his dream. Looking back, how did he view that loss (verses 2-7)?

2. What does David's reflection teach us about God's involvement in our lives?

3. What perspective does David's example give you on any disappointments you are facing or have faced in your life?

4. How do our losses and pain provide opportunities for God's work to be revealed through us?

5. What is the emphasis of David's charge to Solomon and the people in verses 8 and 9? What does this charge tell us about the importance God should have in our everyday lives?

6. Why is it important for us to know that we can hide nothing from God?

7. What did David want Solomon to understand about God in order to serve Him with wholehearted devotion and a willing mind (verse 9)?

8. What impact has seeking God and His will had on your life?

Read 1 Chronicles 28:11-21.

9. What is significant about the fact that the Lord chose Solomon—and not David—to build the temple? How do you think this sovereign choice would contribute to Solomon's success?

10. According to verses 12 and 19, how did David receive the plans for the temple? What does this reveal about how God's man should approach the big projects or decisions of his life?

11. Do you find it easy or difficult to hear the voice of God's Spirit when you need guidance? What can you do to make it easier to hear His voice?

12. In what ways does it encourage you to have God's specific direction through His Word?

13. Why do you think David encouraged Solomon not to be afraid (verse 20)? According to this verse, what is the practical remedy for fear?

14. In verse 21, what additional resources did the Lord put at Solomon's disposal?

15. If you knew that God had called you for a purpose, and you believed that He had already prepared the resources necessary to accomplish the work, how willing would you be to answer His call? Explain.

16. What, if anything, do you think is holding you back and keeping you from realizing God's purpose for your life?

Connect with the Group

Group Opener

Read the group opener aloud and discuss the questions that follow.

When Denise and I (Todd) were first married, we helped lead a Sunday-school class for young married couples. We teamed up with a few other couples, including my older sister, Judi, and her husband, Bob. We were determined to finish strong in our marriages and knew we couldn't do it alone. One of our most successful series was called Marriage from a Twenty-, Thirty-, Forty-, and Fifty-Year Perspective. Godly married couples were invited to share with our class how they survived so many years of marriage and still remained friends. It was hugely popular. As they shared their war stories and secrets to a fulfilling marriage, we all listened intently. We have never forgotten some of their stories and insights that have helped Denise and me stay the course for sixteen years. I remember the insights each couple shared about what they did to keep their marriages alive and how they worked through conflict. We picked up some creative ideas for keeping our marriage strong, and we heard some serious warnings about how to handle conflict and finances. Though marriage is tough, it's not impossible. I keep reminding myself that if these couples can do it, so can we. God wants us to finish strong in our marriages. In fact, He wants us to finish strong in every area of our lives.

Marriage is one area of a man's life that challenges him daily to finish strong. God is committed to helping us finish strong. Philippians 1:6 says, "For I am confident of this very thing, that He who began a good work in you will perfect it until the day of Christ Jesus" (NASB). As I look back, some of the couples who joined us for that class didn't finish well. This is a constant reminder to me that I need God's help to finish strong in every area of my life.

Finishing strong means persevering even when we blow it. Proverbs 24:16 is a great verse that helps me keep getting back up when I fall: "For though a righteous man falls seven times, he rises again, but the wicked are brought down by calamity." In God's mind, stumbling is expected, but rising after a fall is what makes the man.

In what areas of your life are you finishing well? In the areas of your life where you have blown it, have you gotten back up to finish strong?

Discussion Questions

a. Why do men sometimes fail to finish well? When, if ever, have you not finished something well? Explain. What did you learn from the experience?

b. Do you think David finished well from God's point of view? Why or why not?

c. Why do you think David chose to talk more about the temple than about any other aspect of his reign?

d. What can we learn from David's example about how we should deal with the loss of our dreams?

e. What is the most significant lesson you have learned in today's session or from the entire study? Explain your answer.

f. What are you going to do differently as a result of studying the life of David?

Standing Strong

Complete the following sentence based on what you have learned this week about finishing well.

The man after God's own heart _____.

What do you need to do to ensure that at the end of your life God will consider you a man after His own heart?

concluding exercise

What have you learned in this study about how to handle success in a godly way that will help you finish strong? Take a few moments to record your thoughts.

small-group resources

What if men aren't doing the Connect with the Word section before our small-group session?

Don't be discouraged. You set the pace. If you are doing the study and regularly referring to it in conversations with your men through-out the week, they will pick up on its importance. Here are some suggestions to motivate the men in your group to do their home Bible study:

- Send out a midweek e-mail in which you share your answer to one of the study questions. This shows them that you are personally committed to and involved in the study.
- Ask the guys to hit "respond to all" on their e-mail program and share one insight from that week's Bible study with the entire group. Encourage them to send it out before the next small-group session.
- Every time you meet, ask each man in the group to share one insight from his home study.

What if men are not showing up for small group?

This might mean they are losing a sin battle and don't want to admit it to the group. Or they might be consumed with other priorities. Or maybe they don't think they're getting anything out of the group. Here are some suggestions for getting the guys back each week:

- Affirm them when they show up, and tell them how much it means to you that they make small group a priority.

- From time to time, ask them to share one reason they think small group is important to them.
- Regularly call or send out an e-mail the day before you meet to remind them you're looking forward to seeing them.
- Check in with any guy who has missed more than one session, and find out what's going on in his life.
- Get some feedback from the men. You may need to adjust your style. Listen and learn.

What if group discussion is not happening?

You are a discussion facilitator. You have to keep guys involved in the discussion or you'll lose them. You can engage a man who isn't sharing by saying, "Chuck, you've been quiet. What do you think about this question or discussion?" You should also be prepared to share your own personal stories that are related to the discussion questions. You'll set the example by the kind of sharing you do.

What if one man is dominating the group time?

You have to deal with it. If you don't, men will stop showing up. No one wants to hear from just one guy all the time. It will quickly kill morale. Meet with the guy in person and privately. Firmly but gently suggest that he allow others more time to talk. Be positive and encouraging, but truthful. You might say, "Bob, I notice how enthusiastic you are about the group and how you're always prepared to share your thoughts with the group. But there are some pretty quiet guys in the group too. Have you noticed? Would you be willing to help me get them involved in speaking up?"

How do I get the guys in my group more involved?

Give them something to do. Ask one guy to bring a snack. Invite another to lead the prayer time (ask in advance). Have one guy sub for you one week as the leader. (Meet with him beforehand to walk through the group program and the time allotments for each segment.) Encourage another guy to lead a subgroup.

What if guys are not being vulnerable during the Standing Strong or prayer times?

You model openness. You set the pace. Honesty breeds honesty. Vulnerability breeds vulnerability. Are you being vulnerable and honest about your own problems and struggles? (This doesn't mean that you have to spill your guts each week or reveal every secret of your life.) Remember, men want an honest, on-their-level leader who strives to walk with God. (Also, as the leader, you need an accountability partner, perhaps another group leader.)

What will we do at the first session?

We encourage you to open by discussing the **Small-Group Covenant** we've included in this resource section. Ask the men to commit to the study, and then discuss how long it will take your group to complete each session. (We suggest 75-90 minute sessions.) Men find it harder to come up with excuses for missing a group session if they have made a covenant to the other men right at the start.

Begin to identify ways certain men can play a more active role in small group. Give away responsibility. You won't feel as burdened, and your men will grow from the experience. Keep in mind that this process can take a few weeks. Challenge men to fulfill one of the group roles identified later in this resource section. If no one steps forward to fill a role, say to one of the men, "George, I've noticed that you are comfortable praying in a group. Would you lead us each week during that time?"

How can we keep the group connected after we finish a study?
Begin talking about starting another Bible study before you finish this eight-week study. (There are six studies to choose from in the Every Man Bible study series.) Consider having a social time at the conclusion of the study, and encourage the men to invite a friend. This will help create momentum and encourage growth as you launch into another study with your group. There are probably many men in your church or neighborhood who aren't in small groups but would like to be. Be the kind of group that includes others.

As your group grows, consider choosing an apprentice leader who can take half the group into another room for the **Connect with the Group** time. That subgroup can stay together for prayer, or you can reconvene as a large group during that time. You could also meet for discussion as a large group, and then break into subgroups for **Standing Strong** and **prayer**.

If your group doubles in size, it might be a perfect opportunity to release your apprentice leader with half the group to start another group. Allow men to pray about this and make a decision as a group. Typically, the relational complexities that come into play when a small group births a new group work themselves out. Allow guys to choose which group they'd like to be a part of. If guys are slow in choosing one group or another, ask them individually to select one of the groups. Take the lead in making this happen.

Look for opportunities for your group to serve in the church or community. Consider a local outreach project or a short-term missions trip. There are literally hundreds of practical ways you can serve the Lord in outreach. Check with your church leaders to learn the needs in your congregation or community. Create some interest by sending out scouts who will return with a report for the group. Serving keeps men from becoming self-focused and ingrown. When you serve as a group, you will grow as a group.

using this study in a large-group format

Many church leaders are looking for biblically based curriculum that can be used in a large-group setting, such as a Sunday-school class, or for small groups within an existing larger men's group. Each of the Every Man Bible studies can be adapted for this purpose. In addition, this curriculum can become a catalyst for churches wishing to launch men's small groups or to build a men's ministry in their church.

Getting Started

Begin by getting the word out to men in your church, inviting them to join you for a men's study based on one of the topics in the Every Man Bible study series. You can place a notice in your church bulletin, have the pastor announce it from the pulpit, or pursue some other means of attracting interest.

Orientation Week

Arrange your room with round tables and chairs. Put approximately six chairs at each table.

Start your class in prayer and introduce your topic with a short but motivational message from any of the scriptures used in the Bible study. Hand out the curriculum and challenge the men to do their homework before each class. During this first session give the men some discussion questions based upon an overview of the material and have them talk things through just within their small group around the table.

Just before you wrap things up, have each group select a table host or leader. You can do this by having everyone point at once to the person at their table they feel would best facilitate discussion for future meetings.

Ask those newly elected table leaders to stay after for a few minutes, and offer them an opportunity to be further trained as small-group leaders as they lead discussions throughout the course of the study.

Subsequent Weeks

Begin in prayer. Then give a short message (15-25 minutes) based upon the scripture used for that lesson. Pull out the most motivating topics or points and strive to make the discussion relevant to the life of an everyday man and his world. Then leave time for each table to work through the discussion questions listed in the curriculum. Be sure the discussion facilitators at each table close in prayer.

At the end of the eight sessions, you might want to challenge each "table group" to become a small group, inviting them to meet regularly with their new small-group leader and continue building the relationships they've begun.

prayer request record

Date:
Name:
Prayer Request:
Praise:

Date:
Name:
Prayer Request:
Praise:

Date:
Name:
Prayer Request:
Praise:

Date:
Name:
Prayer Request:
Praise:

Date:
Name:
Prayer Request:
Praise:

defining group roles

Group Leader: Leads the lesson and facilitates group discussion.

Apprentice Leader: Assists the leader as needed, which may include leading the lesson.

Refreshment Coordinator: Maintains a list of who will provide refreshments. Calls group members on the list to remind them to bring what they signed up for.

Prayer Warrior: Serves as the contact person for prayer between sessions. Establishes a list of those willing to pray for needs that arise. Maintains the prayer-chain list and activates the chain as needed by calling the first person on the list.

Social Chairman: Plans any desired social events during group sessions or at another scheduled time. Gathers members for planning committees as needed.

small-group roster

Name:
Address:
Phone: E-mail:

Name:
Address:
Phone: E-mail:

Name:
Address:
Phone: E-mail:

Name:
Address:
Phone: E-mail:

Name:
Address:
Phone: E-mail:

Name:
Address:
Phone: E-mail:

spiritual checkup

Your answers to the statements below will help you determine which areas you need to work on in order to grow spiritually. Mark the appropriate letter to the left of each statement. Then make a plan to take one step toward further growth in each area. Don't forget to pray for the Lord's wisdom before you begin. Be honest. Don't be overly critical or rationalize your weaknesses.

Y = Yes
S = Somewhat or Sometimes
N = No

My Spiritual Connection with Other Believers

___I am developing relationships with Christian friends.

___I have joined a small group.

___I am dealing with conflict in a biblical manner.

___I have become more loving and forgiving than I was a year ago.

___I am a loving and devoted husband and father.

My Spiritual Growth

___I have committed to daily Bible reading and prayer.

___I am journaling on a regular basis, recording my spiritual growth.

____I am growing spiritually by studying the Bible with others.

____I am honoring God in my finances and personal giving.

____I am filled with joy and gratitude for my life, even during trials.

____I respond to challenges with peace and faith instead of anxiety and anger.

____I avoid addictive behaviors (excessive drinking, overeating, watching too much TV, etc.).

Serving Christ and Others

____I am in the process of discovering my spiritual gifts and talents.

____I am involved in ministry in my church.

____I have taken on a role or responsibility in my small group.

____I am committed to helping someone else grow in his spiritual walk.

Sharing Christ with Others

____I care about and am praying for those around me who are unbelievers.

____I share my experience of coming to know Christ with others.

____I invite others to join me in this group or for weekend worship services.

____I am seeing others come to Christ and am praying for this to happen.

____I do what I can to show kindness to people who don't know Christ.

Surrendering My Life for Growth

___I attend church services weekly.

___I pray for others to know Christ, and I seek to fulfill the Great Commission.

___I regularly worship God through prayer, praise, and music, both at church and at home.

___I care for my body through exercise, nutrition, and rest.

___I am concerned about using my energy to serve God's purposes instead of my own.

My Identity in the Lord

___I see myself as a beloved son of God, one whom God loves regardless of my sin.

___I can come to God in all of my humanity and know that He accepts me completely. When I fail, I willingly run to God for forgiveness.

___I experience Jesus as an encouraging Friend and Lord each moment of the day.

___I have an abiding sense that God is on my side. I am aware of His gracious presence with me throughout the day.

___During moments of beauty, grace, and human connection, I lift up praise and thanks to God.

___I believe that using my talents to their fullest pleases the Lord.

___I experience God's love for me in powerful ways.

small-group covenant

As a committed group member, I agree to the following:*

- **Regular Attendance.** I will attend group sessions on time and let everyone know in advance if I can't make it.
- **Group Safety.** I will help create a safe, encouraging environment where men can share their thoughts and feelings without fear of embarrassment or rejection. I will not judge another guy or attempt to fix his problems.
- **Confidentiality.** I will always keep to myself everything that is shared in the group.
- **Acceptance.** I will respect different opinions or beliefs and let Scripture be the teacher.
- **Accountability.** I will make myself accountable to the other group members for the personal goals I share.
- **Friendliness.** I will look for those around me who might join the group and explore their faith with other men.
- **Ownership.** I will prayerfully consider taking on a specific role within the group as the opportunity arises.
- **Spiritual Growth.** I will commit to establishing a daily quiet time with God, which includes doing the homework for this study. I will share with the group the progress I make and the struggles I experience as I seek to grow spiritually.

Signed: _____ Date: _____

---

* *Permission is given to photocopy and distribute this form to each man in your group. Review this covenant quarterly or as needed.*

about the authors

 STEPHEN ARTERBURN is coauthor of the best-selling Every Man series. He is also founder and chairman of New Life Clinics, host of the daily *New Life Live!* national radio program, and creator of the Women of Faith conferences. A nationally known speaker and licensed minister, Stephen has authored more than forty books. He lives with his family in Laguna Beach, California.

 KENNY LUCK is president and founder of Every Man Ministries and coauthor of *Every Man, God's Man* and its companion workbook. He is division leader for men's small groups and teaches a men's interactive Bible study at Saddleback Church in Lake Forest, California. He and his wife, Chrissy, have three children and reside in Rancho Santa Margarita, California.

 TODD WENDORFF is a graduate of U.C. Berkeley and holds a Th.M. from Talbot School of Theology. He serves as a pastor of men's ministries at Saddleback Church and is an adjunct professor at Biola University. He is an author of the Doing Life Together Bible study series. Todd and his wife, Denise, live with their three children in Trabuco Canyon, California.

every man's battle workshops

from New Life Ministries

new Life Ministries receives hundreds of calls every month from Christian men who are struggling to stay pure in the midst of daily challenges to their sexual integrity and from pastors who are looking for guidance in how to keep fragile marriages from falling apart all around them.

As part of our commitment to equip individuals to win these battles, New Life Ministries has developed biblically based workshops directly geared to answer these needs. These workshops are held several times per year around the country.

- Our workshops for men are structured to equip men with the tools necessary to maintain sexual integrity and enjoy healthy, productive relationships.

- Our workshops for church leaders are targeted to help pastors and men's ministry leaders develop programs to help families being attacked by this destructive addiction.

Some comments from previous workshop attendees:

"An awesome, life-changing experience. Awesome teaching, teacher, content and program." —DAVE

"God has truly worked a great work in me since the EMB workshop. I am fully confident that with God's help, I will be restored in my ministry position. Thank you for your concern. I realize that this is a battle, but I now have the weapons of warfare as mentioned in Ephesians 6:10, and I am using them to gain victory!" —KEN

"It's great to have a workshop you can confidently recommend to anyone without hesitation, knowing that it is truly life changing. Your labors are not in vain!" —DR. BRAD STENBERG, Pasadena, CA

If sexual temptation is threatening your marriage or your church, please call **1-800-NEW-LIFE** to speak with one of our specialists.